Big and Little

PROGRAM AUTHORS
Richard L. Allington
Ronald L. Cramer
Patricia M. Cunningham
G. Yvonne Pérez
Constance Frazier Robinson
Robert J. Tierney

PROGRAM CONSULTANTS
Bernadine J. Bolden
Ann Hall
Sylvia M. Lee
Dolores Perez
Jo Ann Wong

CRITIC READERS
Maria P. Barela
Phinnize J. Brown
Jean C. Carter
Nancy Peterson
Nancy Welsh
Kay Williams

John C. Manning, *Instructional Consultant*

SCOTT, FORESMAN AND COMPANY
Editorial Offices: Glenview, Illinois

Regional Offices: Sunnyvale, California •
Tucker, Georgia • Glenview, Illinois •
Oakland, New Jersey • Dallas, Texas

ACKNOWLEDGMENTS

Text
"I Like You" by Masuhito. From *I Like You and Other Poems for Valentine's Day*, edited by Yaroslava. Charles Scribner's Sons, 1976.

Artist
Hockerman, Dennis: Pages 6–31, 34–63

Photographs
Scott, Foresman & Co.: Pages 32–33

Cover Artist
Dennis Hockerman

ISBN 0-673-72649-5

1991 printing
Copyright © 1988, 1985

Scott, Foresman and Company, A Division of Harper Collins *Publishers*. Glenview, Illinois. All Rights Reserved. Printed in the United States of America.

2

Contents

Stories by: Katy Hall

Big and Little

Making Friends Happy

A Hat for Mouse

Bear gives a hat to Mouse.

Bear gives a blue hat to Mouse.

Mouse has a blue hat.

8   UNIT 1

Elephant gives a hat to Mouse.

Elephant gives a yellow hat to Mouse.

Mouse has a little yellow hat.

Mouse has a long, long blue hat.

Mouse gives the long hat to Elephant.

Mouse gives the long blue hat to Elephant.

Elephant has the long blue hat.

Mouse has the little yellow hat.

Elephant likes the long blue hat.

Mouse likes the little yellow hat.

Elephant likes Mouse.

Mouse likes Elephant.

The Good Laugh

Mouse has a funny book.

The funny book makes Mouse laugh.

Mouse likes to laugh.

Mouse has a good laugh.

Mouse likes to read funny books.

Mouse can read the funny

book to Elephant.

Mouse has a good laugh.

Can Elephant laugh?

Mouse plays music for Elephant.

Mouse has a good laugh.

Can Elephant laugh?

Mouse can paint a funny elephant.

Elephant likes the funny elephant.

Mouse has a good laugh.

Elephant has a good laugh.

Elephant can laugh!

Learning to Play

Kick the Ball

Elephant has a ball.

The ball is big.

Elephant is big.

Elephant kicks the ball to a tree .

Mouse has the ball.

The ball is big.

Mouse is little.

Can Mouse kick the big ball?

Can Mouse kick the ball to the tree ?

The ball is big.

Mouse is little.

Mouse can not kick the big ball.

Elephant kicks the ball.

Elephant kicks the ball for Mouse.

Elephant kicks the ball in the tree !

Who Will Keep the Ball?

Mouse likes to run.

Mouse likes to play ball.

Bear will not give the ball to Mouse.

Bear likes to keep the ball.

Elephant likes to run.

Elephant likes to play ball.

Bear will not give the ball to Elephant.

Bear likes to keep the ball.

Mouse can not play ball.

Elephant can not play ball.

Bear likes to keep the ball.

Will Bear keep the ball?

Bear sees a  beehive .

Bear runs to the beehive .

Will Mouse run to the ball?

Will Elephant run to the ball?

The  bees see Bear.

Bear runs.

Bear will not play.

Bear will not keep the ball.

Elephant has the ball.

Mouse has the ball.

Elephant will keep the ball!

Mouse will keep the ball!

Who Likes Mouse?

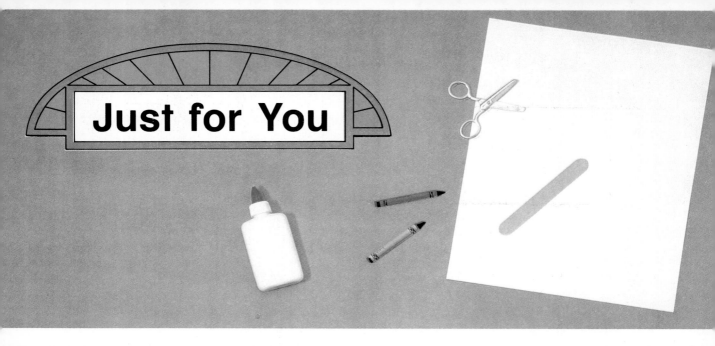

Just for You

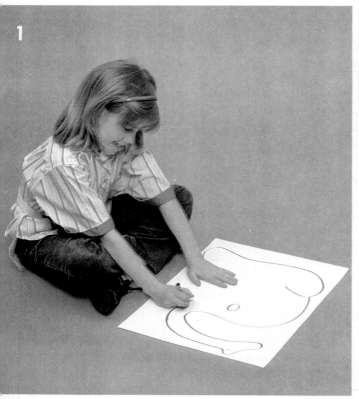

1

2

Working Together

The Blue and Yellow Kite

Mouse has a kite.

The kite is blue and yellow.

Mouse likes the blue and yellow kite.

 I want to fly the kite, Mouse!

I want to make the kite fly and fly!

 I want the kite, Elephant.

I want to make the kite fly.

 I can fly the blue and yellow kite!

I can fly the kite to the sun!

 The kite is in the  !

Is the bat in the  ?

 **The bat is in the**  **cave** .

 The bat has the kite!

I want the kite!

Come to the  Cave

 Come, Mouse.

Come to the  cave .

You want the kite.

I will give the kite to you.

 Elephant, you go with the bat.

Go in the cave with the bat.

The bat will give the kite to you.

A mouse is like a bat.

Mouse, you go with the bat.

Go in the  cave with the bat.

The bat will give the kite to you.

Mouse and Elephant, come in!

 I will go in with you, Elephant.

 I will go in with you, Mouse.

 Come in, come in!

The bat gives the kite to Mouse.

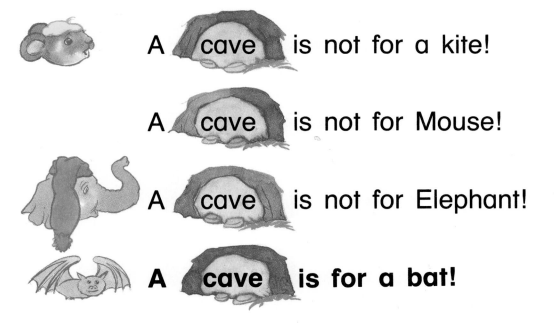

A cave is not for a kite!

A cave is not for Mouse!

A cave is not for Elephant!

A cave is for a bat!

Fun at the Lake

The Lake

Come to the lake, Mouse.

Come to the lake to eat.

I like the lake.

I like to eat.

I will go with you.

Mouse runs to the lake with Elephant.

Mouse has a big red apple.

The red apple is big for Mouse.

 My red apple is big.

 I will keep the apple for you.

Mouse gives the apple to Elephant.

Mouse and Elephant run to the lake.

 I like to go to the lake to

eat apples.

 I want to eat my big red apple.

Mouse sees the apple.

 I can not eat my red apple!

 Eat my little apples, Mouse.

Mouse will not eat the big red apple.

Mouse will eat little apples.

The Funny Boat Ride

 See the  raccoon in the boat!

I want to ride in the boat.

 You ride in the boat.

I want to eat cake.

 You eat cake.

I want to jump into the boat.

I want to ride with the  raccoon .

Come jump into my boat.

Jump into my boat for a ride.

Elephant, come eat the cake in

my boat.

Come jump into my boat.

Mouse and Elephant jump into the boat.

Elephant can not jump with the cake.

Elephant sees the cake fly!

My cake is into the lake!

I want my cake.

Elephant jumps into the lake.

Elephant eats some funny cake.

I will eat my cake.

Mouse, you ride in the boat.

Mouse and the raccoon laugh.

Come Ride with Elephant

 I want to go for a ride.

Can you fly the funny  plane ?

 I can fly the funny  plane .

Come for a ride.

Elephant jumps in.

Mouse is little.

Mouse can not jump in.

Will Mouse go for a ride?

Mouse will go with Elephant.

Mouse will go for a ride in the

funny  plane .

Who will Mouse and Elephant see?

 I see Bear and the bat.

I see the boat and the lake!

I see my house and the cave !

 I like to fly a funny plane .

 I like to ride in a funny plane .

I Like You

by Masuhito

Although I saw you
The day before yesterday,
   And yesterday and today,
   This much is true—
I want to see you tomorrow, too!

Word List

The words below are listed by unit. Following each word is the page of first appearance of the word.

Unit 1, 6-17

hat 8
mouse 8
gives 8
elephant 9
long 9
good 12
laugh 12
funny 12

Unit 2, 18-33

kick 18
ball 18
is 18

not 20
will 22
keep 22
run 22

Unit 3, 34-45

and 36
kite 36
I 37
want 37
fly 37
bat 39
come 41
you 41

go 42
with 42

Unit 4, 46-63

lake 48
eat 48
red 49
apple 49
my 50
boat 53
ride 53
cake 53
jump 54
into 54

Books to Read

One Sun by Bruce McMillan
Have fun with words that sound alike!